Science Experiments

WATER

by
John Farndon

Benchmark Books

MARSHALL CAVENDISH
NEW YORK

Marshall Cavendish Corporation

99 White Plains Road

Tarrytown, New York 10591-9001

© Marshall Cavendish Corporation, 2001

Created by Brown Partworks Ltd

Library of Congress Cataloging-in-Publication Data

Farndon, John

    Water / by John Farndon
    p. cm. — (Science experiments)
    Includes index.
    ISBN 0-7614-1087-2
    1. Water—Experiments—Juvenile literature. [1. Water—Experiments.
2. Experiments.] I. Title.

CIP Data available at the Library of Congress

Printed in Hong Kong

PHOTOGRAPHIC CREDITS

t – top; b – bottom; c – center; l – left; r – right

Corbis - title page, Liba Taylor (c); p4, Liba Taylor (bl); p4, 5 (b); p7,
Wolfgang Kaehler (tr); p22, 23 Gary Braasch (b); p26 Philip James Corwin
(b)
David Noble - p10, (b); p15 (tr)
The Image Bank - p6 Tom Mareschal (b)
Leslie Garland - p24 (br)
Pictor - p27 (br)
Stock Shot - p14, 15 Tony Harrington (b)
Travel Ink - p18, 19 Angela Hampton (b); p19 Stephen Andrews (tr)

Step-by-step photography throughout: Martin Norris

Front cover: Martin Norris

Contents

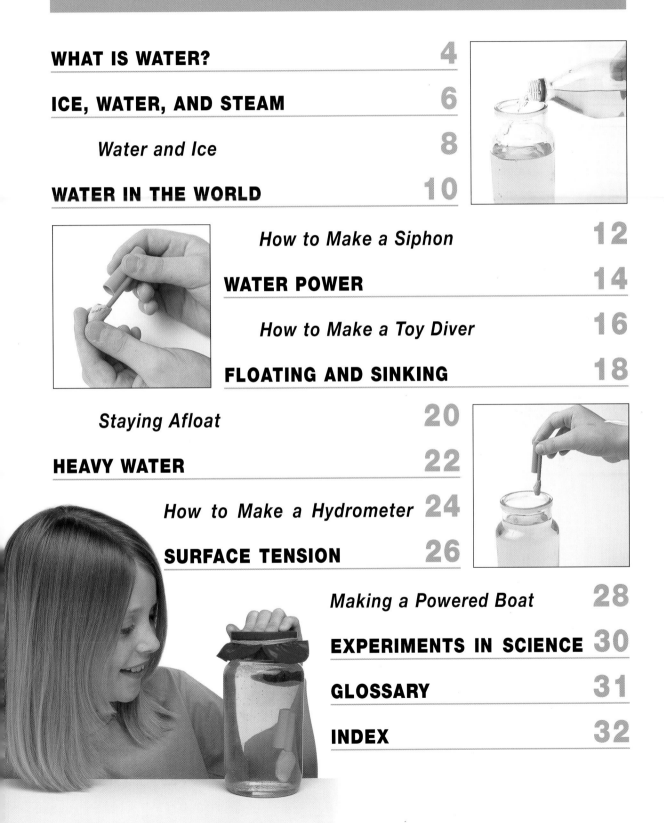

WHAT IS WATER? 4

ICE, WATER, AND STEAM 6

Water and Ice 8

WATER IN THE WORLD 10

How to Make a Siphon 12

WATER POWER 14

How to Make a Toy Diver 16

FLOATING AND SINKING 18

Staying Afloat 20

HEAVY WATER 22

How to Make a Hydrometer 24

SURFACE TENSION 26

Making a Powered Boat 28

EXPERIMENTS IN SCIENCE 30

GLOSSARY 31

INDEX 32

WHAT IS WATER?

*W*ater is so common on Earth that we almost take it for granted. It is by far the most common substance on the face of the earth, and you can find it almost everywhere. Water covers almost three-quarters of the world's surface.

Water fills the oceans, rivers, and lakes. It is in the ground. It is in the air we breathe. It is in our bodies. It is fortunate that water is so common, because water is vital to life. There are no living things on Earth that can survive without a

A view of our planet from space shows a world that is largely covered by water.

Did you know?

THE NEED FOR WATER

Humans can live without food for more than two months, but they can only survive without water for about a week. If the body loses more than 20 percent of its normal water content, a person will die. Humans need about 2½ quarts (2.4 liters) of water a day. This intake can be in the form of beverages or water in food.

regular supply of water. If you let a houseplant dry out, it wilts and dies very quickly. In fact, every living thing consists mostly of water. Your body is about two-thirds water. Many plants are about four-fifths water. Most scientists believe that life itself began in water—in the salty water of the sea.

In the real world

Scientists once thought water was an element, one of the basic chemicals of the universe. In fact, water is a compound (combination) of two gases—oxygen and hydrogen. This was first discovered in 1783 by British scientist Henry Cavendish.

Cavendish used a spark to set fire to a mixture of air and hydrogen gas inside a glass jar. The hydrogen burned up quickly, but Cavendish saw that drops of water had formed on the glass. When he weighed the jar he found that it weighed exactly the same as it had at the start of the experiment.

Cavendish realized that the hydrogen had not escaped at all. In fact, it had joined with oxygen in the air to form water. Careful measurement showed Cavendish that water was made from twice as much hydrogen as oxygen. This is why water has the chemical formula H_2O.

ICE, WATER, AND STEAM

When liquid water is heated, it boils. The water turns into a gas called water vapor. When the vapor molecules meet cold air, some form tiny droplets of liquid. We see these droplets as steam.

Did you know?

People often confuse steam and water vapor. Water vapor is the gas formed when water evaporates completely and is invisible. Steam is the tiny drops of water that you can see drifting up off hot water.

In the real world

Water expands when it freezes, so a certain volume of water freezes to make a larger volume of ice. This means that ice is actually less dense (lighter) than water, so ice floats on water. This is why when chunks of ice snap off the end of glaciers into the Arctic Ocean, they do not sink. Instead, they float away as large chunks of ice called icebergs. Because ice is only slightly less dense than water, the iceberg sinks deep into the water. Only the very tip of the iceberg shows above the surface. This makes icebergs very dangerous for ships that accidentally bump into them, like the *Titanic*, which sank when it hit an iceberg on its first voyage in 1912.

If it gets cold enough, liquid water freezes and turns to solid ice. If it gets hot enough, water boils and turns into a gas called water vapor.

This is one of the special things about water. Other substances turn from solid to liquid and from liquid to gas if they are heated. For most materials, this only happens at extreme temperatures. Iron, for instance, does not melt until the temperature is over 2,732°F (1,500°C). It does not boil until the temperature soars over a roasting 4,892°F (2,700°C).

Water changes from solid to liquid to gas at everyday temperatures. Pure water melts at 32°F (0°C) and boils at 212°F (100°C). If there are any impurities, the melting and boiling points change. This is one way of testing to see if a liquid is pure water.

Did you know?

SPECIAL BONDS

Water stays liquid until it gets very warm. A lot of energy has to be added to liquid water before the molecules can break apart and form a gas. The reason water stays liquid for so long is because pairs of its molecules are held together by special bonds. These bonds are called hydrogen bonds. Just as opposite poles of a magnet attract each other, the opposite sides of two water molecules stick together (see the box on page 8). Only when it gets very warm do these bonds break apart, allowing water to turn to gas.

WATER AND ICE

You will need

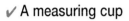

- ✔ A refrigerator with a freezer
- ✔ A strong plastic cup and saucer
- ✔ A heavy weight, large enough to rest on the cup
- ✔ A measuring cup

1 Using the measuring cup, fill the plastic cup to the brim with water. Rest the cup on the saucer.

In focus

WATER MOLECULES

A molecule of water is the tiniest bit of water that exists. Each water molecule has two hydrogen atoms and one oxygen atom. A water molecule is shaped like a flattened V, with the two hydrogen atoms on each tip and the oxygen atom in the middle. Scientists describe water molecules as polar. This is because one "pole" or side of the molecule, the oxygen side, has a slightly negative electrical charge. The other side has a slightly positive electrical charge. The attractions between the positive pole on one molecule and the negative pole on another molecule are called hydrogen bonds.

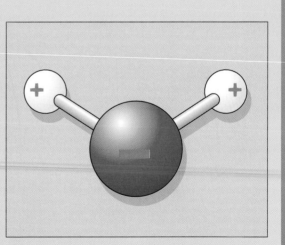

This diagram shows the V-shape of a water molecule. The oxygen atom is shown in red, and the two hydrogen atoms in white.

What is happening?

When most substances freeze from liquid to solid, they shrink. Unlike most other substances, water expands as it freezes. In other words, a certain volume of water freezes to make a slightly larger volume of ice, which is why the ice fills the jug higher than the water. In fact, when it freezes, water swells with enormous power—enough power to lift the weight. This can cause a problem in household water pipes. In cold winters, water can expand inside pipes as it freezes and burst the pipes.

2 Place the weight on top of the cup. Now carefully carry the cup and saucer and put them inside the freezer.

Leave overnight, then take the cup out of the freezer. You will see that the ice has lifted the weight above the edge of the cup.

WATER IN THE WORLD

Nearly all the water in the world, 97.25 percent, is the salt water of the oceans. Most of the rest of the world's water, 2.05 percent, is locked away in the frozen polar ice caps and in glaciers. Less than 1 percent of the water on Earth is freshwater in lakes and rivers, springs, and under ground. An even tinier proportion exists as rain, snow, and water vapor in the air.

Most freshwater lies under the ground. Only about 0.02 percent of freshwater is found in rivers and lakes.

Did you know?

If you have ever tasted seawater, you know it tastes salty. This is because seawater is only 96.5 percent pure water. Dissolved in it, like sugar in a cup of coffee, are billions of tons of salts. By far the most common salt is sodium chloride, table salt. Seawater also contains other ingredients such as magnesium, sulfur, calcium, and potassium.

Most ocean water stays in the oceans, circulating round and round as the ocean waters are warmed by the Sun and blown by the wind.

Freshwater is continually changing places, moving among the oceans, the air, and the land in an endless cycle. The technical word for anything to do with water is hydrology, and scientists call this cycle of freshwater the hydrological cycle or water cycle.

In the real world

WATER NEEDS

There is a huge amount of water in the world. But the human need for water is great, and the water does not always exist where it is needed. As the world's population grows, our need for water grows too. In the year 2000, the world demand for freshwater was almost double what it was in the 1980s. Rich countries such as the United States and those in Europe use huge amounts of water. The average European uses 6,340 pints (3,000 liters) of water a day; the average African uses just 4.2 pints (2 liters). Some countries regularly suffer droughts and water shortages, and no country is completely safe from finding itself short of water.

In focus

THE HYDROLOGICAL CYCLE

The world's freshwater is being recycled all the time. Every second of the day, a huge amount of new water vapor is joining the air as it evaporates from oceans and lakes or transpires from plants. Warm air currents then lift the vapor high up where the air gets cooler. As the air cools, the vapor condenses (turns to drops of water) or freezes into tiny ice crystals, forming clouds. The water drops and ice crystals in clouds grow bigger as more water vapor floats up. Soon they grow so big they become too heavy to float on the air, and they fall back to the ground or into the oceans as rain or snow. This is called precipitation. When rain or snow falls on the ground, it either soaks in and is taken up by plants, or it runs in rivers back to lakes and the oceans, ready to evaporate again.

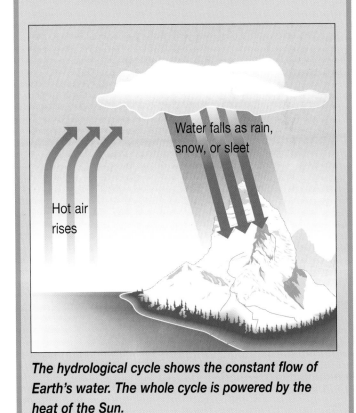

Water falls as rain, snow, or sleet

Hot air rises

The hydrological cycle shows the constant flow of Earth's water. The whole cycle is powered by the heat of the Sun.

HOW TO MAKE A SIPHON

You will need

- ✓ A length of clean, flexible plastic tube about 2 to 3 ft (0.6 to 1 m) long.
- ✓ Two large plastic bottles
- ✓ A jug

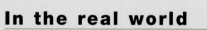

1 Set up the bottles on a waterproof table, or outdoors. Then fill one bottle with water from the jug.

In the real world

IRRIGATION SYSTEMS

Growing crops need huge amounts of water. It takes around 20,000 pints (10,000 liters) of water to grow every 2 lbs (1 kg) of food. In dry countries, there is often not enough water for crops to thrive. Even in less arid countries, farmers may need more water to boost crop production. Many farmers channel water onto the land. This is called irrigation. In recent years, more and more farmland has been irrigated, especially in Asia. A fifth of the world's cropland is now irrigated, and this land produces over a third of the world's food.

3 Lift the bottle above shoulder height. Stop sucking and clamp your thumb over the end of the tube.

What is happening?

The empty bottle drinks from the full bottle in a process called siphoning. The siphon works because the pressure of water in the full bottle is greater than it is in the empty bottle. The difference in pressure drives the water through the tube. The siphon will stop when the water in each bottle is at the same height and the pressure is equal.

2 Dip one end of the tube in the full bottle. Take a deep breath and suck the water through the tube to fill it.

Place the end of the tube in the empty bottle, taking your thumb away as you do. You will see at once that the empty water bottle starts drinking water from the full bottle.

In focus

PUMPS

Siphons only work when there is a difference in water pressure, which means they only work "downhill." To lift water up, you need a pump. The simplest pumps are old-fashioned hand pumps, which date back to at least 300 B.C. They lift a little water at a time from underground with a plunger or piston moved up and down by a hand lever. Modern motorized pumps use rotating gears or vanes to move the water.

WATER POWER

If you have ever stood under a waterfall or been bowled over by a big wave from the sea, you know that water has immense power when it is moving. Sometimes water's power comes from its momentum. Big waves are very hard to stop because there is such a weight of water in them. Other times water's power comes from its depth, since pressure—the water's power to push—increases with depth. Sometimes the power comes from gravity, as when rivers flow downhill to turn a water wheel or turbine.

The amount of power water generates when it is flowing downhill depends on its pressure. The pressure depends on the weight of water pushing down. Hydrologists talk of a "head" of water. This is really

Surfers are using the power of water when they ride the ocean waves.

In focus

Hydroelectric power (HEP) plants use moving water to turn turbines to generate electricity. Typically a huge dam is constructed. The power plant is often inside the base of the dam, where the pressure is greatest. Sluice gates open to let water gush through a tunnel to the plant's turbine. As the water rushes through the turbine, it spins the turbine blades, and the turbine drives the electric generator.

HEP plants are expensive to build. But once they are working, they are cheaper to run than oil and coal power stations and they do not pollute the air. At present, HEP accounts for about 20 percent of the world's electric power and about 9 percent of the electricity produced in the United States.

In the real world

WATERMILLS

Watermills are the simplest and oldest power plants, dating back at least to the time of the Romans. They have a wheel with paddles that are turned by water flowing either under them (undershot wheels) or over the top (overshot wheels). Until the Industrial Revolution in Britain, watermills were used mainly for grinding corn. They were also used in ancient China to blow bellows for metal-working. When the Industrial Revolution came in the mid-18th century, huge water wheels were used to power machines in the first factories.

Until the invention of the steam engine, people relied on water power. This watermill in France was used to grind corn.

just the depth of water creating the pressure. The deeper the water, the greater the head and the greater the pressure at the bottom. A cubic foot (0.028 cubic m) of water weighs 62.4 pounds (28 kg), so water 100 feet (30.5 m) deep creates a pressure of 62.4 times 100 or 6,240 pounds per square foot at the bottom. Water would shoot out of a pipe through a dam 100 feet below the surface at over 80 feet per second.

To use water power, hydrologists try to create a large head or depth of water by damming up a river in a pond or lake. In old-fashioned watermills, they built a millpond. In modern hydroelectric power plants, they often build a huge dam.

HOW TO MAKE A TOY DIVER

You will need

- ✓ A tall glass jar with a wide neck
- ✓ A small plastic pen cap
- ✓ Thin, strong string
- ✓ A small sheet of thin rubber
- ✓ Re-usable poster putty

1 Fill the jar with water almost to the top. Fix a small lump of poster putty to the tip of the pocket clip on the pen cap to make the pen cap float upright.

In focus

You can see how water pressure increases with depth with this simple experiment. Cut the top off a plastic bottle. Make a row of three holes up the side of the bottle, 2 in (5 cm) apart. Cover the holes tightly with your fingers. Ask a friend to fill the bottle with water. Once the bottle is full, take away your fingers, all at once. The water trickles from the top hole and shoots out farther from the middle. It jets out most powerfully from the lowest hole because the pressure is greatest here.

3 Cut the rubber in a circle about 1¼ in (3 cm) wider than the jar top. Stretch it over the top of the jar and tie it around the neck with the string.

What is happening?

The pen cap and poster putty are kept afloat by the bubble of air trapped inside the cap. When you press on the rubber, you increase the pressure of the water in the bottle. The extra pressure forces extra water into the cap so that it sinks.

Note: Before starting this experiment, block the airhole on the pen cap. Don't forget to unplug it again when you have finished.

2 Float the pen cap, point up, in a bowl of water. Add or remove poster putty until it floats just below the surface. Now lower the cap into the jar.

Press the rubber down into the neck of the jar. Watch what happens to the pen cap. It should slowly sink. Release your fingers and it should float up again.

FLOATING AND SINKING

Some things, such as corks, float on water, while others, such as stones, sink. Objects that float are lighter or less dense than water. Things that sink are heavier or more dense.

Whenever an object is put in water, its weight pushes downward. As the object pushes down, it pushes water out of the way. The water pushes the object back with a force equal to

The air inside this rubber ring is less dense than water so the ring, and the girl, float.

Did you know?

You can lift someone quite heavy when you are standing in a swimming pool, because the upthrust of the water makes them more buoyant.

Our scientific understanding of why things float and why things sink dates back to the brilliant Ancient Greek thinker Archimedes. Archimedes (c.287–212 B.C.) lived in Syracuse in Sicily. He made many important contributions to science, including the theory of levers, and devised many ingenious inventions. It was Archimedes who realized that when an object is immersed in water, its weight pushes down, but the water pushes it back up with a force equal to the weight of water displaced. This is called Archimedes' Principle.

the weight of water displaced (pushed out of the way). This pushing back is called "upthrust." Upthrust makes things lighter in water than they are in air. The loss of weight is called buoyancy.

If the object is less dense than water, the weight of water displaced is greater than the weight of the object. The upthrust pushes the object and makes it float. If the object is more dense than water, the weight of water displaced is less than the weight of the object. The upthrust is too small to keep the object afloat.

Corks float because they are much less dense than water. Steel ships float because although steel is denser than water, the ships' hulls are full of air. They sink until enough water is displaced to match the weight of air in the hull.

FISH AND THEIR SWIMBLADDERS

To keep them afloat, many fish have a special air bag inside their bodies called a swimbladder. Without this, the fish would have to swim all the time to avoid sinking. Sharks and rays have no swimbladder, and they drift slowly to the bottom whenever they stop swimming.

Just as air in a buoyancy ring keeps you afloat in the swimming pool, the gas in a fish's swimbladder helps it float at a particular depth in the sea. As a fish dives deeper, the water pressure increases. The extra water pressure squeezes the gas in the bladder. To avoid sinking the fish inflates the bladder with extra gas made in its blood. When the fish swims higher, the water pressure decreases and the extra gas is let out.

STAYING AFLOAT

You will need

- ✓ A small airtight glass jar, half-filled with water
- ✓ A plastic measuring cup
- ✓ Paper and pen
- ✓ A kitchen scale
- ✓ A larger jar

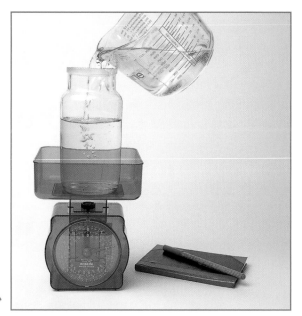

1 Stand the large jar in the pan of the kitchen scale. Fill it exactly to the brim with water, taking care not to spill any water into the scale pan. Note the weight.

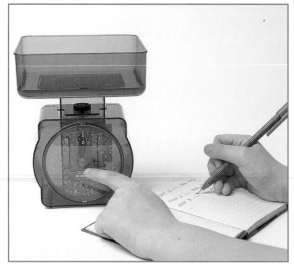

3 Take the large jar out of the pan. Note the weight of water spilled into the pan. This is the water that was displaced by the small jar.

Did you know

THE DEAD SEA

The desert heat makes the waters of the Dead Sea evaporate and turn incredibly salty. The extra salt makes the water so dense that people can float in it as easily as if they were floating on an airbed.

What is happening?

This experiment shows how the weight of water displaced—and so the upthrust—is exactly equal to the weight of the object. You will also find that subtracting either the weight of the water displaced or the weight of the jar from the combined weight in step 2 will give you the original weight that you had in step 1.

2 Gently lower the small jar into the large jar. This will make some water spill out into the scales pan. Note the weight now. The weight has increased.

Now empty the pan and weigh the small jar. You will find the small jar weighs exactly the same as the displaced water.

HEAVY WATER

Just as solids that are less dense than water float, so too do liquids that are less dense—so long as they do not mix. You can often see thin layers of oil shimmering on the surface of puddles in the road. The oil is dropped by trucks and automobiles. It is less dense than water so it floats on rainwater. Liquids that are more dense than water sink.

In the same way, cold water sinks in warm water because cold water is more dense. Warm water floats up in cold water because it is less dense. This can create convection currents. Convection is when warm water is "conveyed," or carried

Oil is lighter than water. It forms a shimmering layer on top of puddles and wet roads.

Did you know?

Nuclear power plants use a special kind of water called "heavy water." Ordinary water molecules are made from oxygen and ordinary hydrogen. Heavy water molecules are made from a special "heavy" kind of hydrogen called deuterium. Heavy water is slightly denser than ordinary water but otherwise much the same. It is very effective at containing nuclear reactions.

upward, in cold water while cold water sinks in another place.

The upward movement of warm water and the downward movement of cold water combine to create a circulation. This circulation is a convection current. You can see small convection currents in water boiling in a saucepan on an electric burner. Convection currents on a much larger scale play an important part in the oceans and in the structure of the earth.

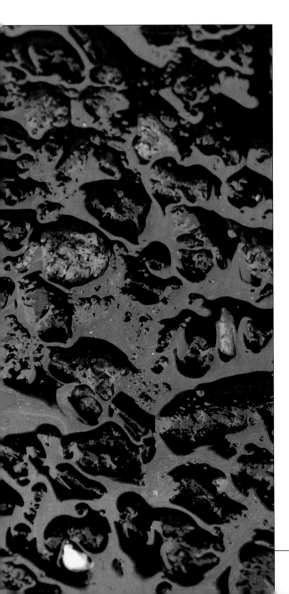

HOW THE WORLD'S DEEP OCEAN CURRENTS WORK

The surface waters of the oceans are circulating round and round all the time because they are blown along by the wind. But the whole ocean is circulating very slowly too, not just the surface water. Slow, deep circulation is driven by differences in the density of seawater. These circulations are called "thermohaline" circulations because the differences in density are created by the temperature and salt content of the water. ("Thermo" means temperature and "haline" means salt.) Cold water is more dense than warm water. Saltier water is more dense than water with a lower concentration of salt. Small changes in density can make large changes in the circulation.

One important thermohaline circulation happens because dense water forms in the polar regions where the air is very cold. Salt is left behind as seawater freezes into ice, making the water here extra dense. Dense water develops like this beneath the Arctic and Antarctic ice sheets, then sinks deep down and spreads slowly out toward the equator.

Surface ocean currents rotate clockwise in the Northern Hemisphere and counterclockwise in the Southern Hemisphere.

HOW TO MAKE A HYDROMETER

You will need

- ✔ Re-usable poster putty
- ✔ Identical drinking glasses
- ✔ Plastic drinking straws
  (check that they float evenly)
- ✔ Cooking oil
- ✔ Marker pen
- ✔ Water
- ✔ Salt

1 Cut each straw in half and make marks across each one at regular intervals. Stick some poster putty on one end of each straw. This is your hydrometer.

In the real world

THE PLIMSOLL LINE

Ships float at different heights if the density of water varies. They float higher in seawater than in freshwater because the salt in seawater makes it dense. They also float higher in dense, cold seas than in warm seas. The higher the ship floats, the more weight it can safely carry. Some ships are marked with lines to show the level to which they can be loaded. There are different lines for tropical water, freshwater, summer, and winter. The lines are called Plimsoll lines after their inventor, English politician Samuel Plimsoll.

2 Pour some water into one glass. Lower a hydrometer, weighted-end first, into the water and let it float upright. Note which mark the water comes to.

3 Fill the second glass with exactly the same amount of water. Add a tablespoon of salt and stir well. Take another reading with a hydrometer.

Fill the third glass with cooking oil and lower a hydrometer into it. Note where the water comes to.

What is happening?

The hydrometer shows how dense a liquid is because it sinks deep into a light liquid like oil and less deep in a heavier one like salt water. Typically, the scale on a hydrometer is set from the height at which the instrument floats in pure water. The densities of other liquids are called "relative densities."

SURFACE TENSION

Bubbles are round because their outside layer is pulled inward by surface tension.

Drops of water are always round. Look at the condensation on a soda can or raindrops hitting a window. They are round because of surface tension.

Surface tension happens because water molecules attract each other. In the middle of a drop, there are lots of molecules pulling toward each other in all directions. At the

surface, molecules are only pulled back into the water, because there are no molecules pulling the other way. So the water pulls its surface tight around it, like a stretchy skin.

Surface tension is quite weak and only pulls small droplets into balls. But it has many effects. It is surface tension that makes the water surface form an arc called a "meniscus" when you fill a glass right to the brim. Surface tension allows small insects, such as pond skaters, to walk on water. It is also surface tension that keeps water from getting through the tiny holes in fabrics such as cotton. This is why tents keep out rain as long as you do not bang the fabric and break the surface tension.

In focus

HOW SOAP WORKS

Water on its own is not much good at cleaning. To remove grease and grime you need to add soap or detergent to the water.

Soaps and detergents clean because their molecules are attracted to both water and grease. One end of the molecule is hydrophilic (meaning water-loving) and is attracted to water. The other end is hydrophobic (water-hating); it likes grease and dirt. The hydrophobic end of the molecule digs its way into the dirt. The hydrophilic end is drawn into the water, and this pulls the dirt away.

Grease often will not wash off surfaces because surface tension in water stops the water from getting into the grease. Detergents often contain special molecules called surfactants. These lower the surface tension, which increases the water's ability to make things wet.

Soaps are made by boiling animal fat or vegetable oil with sodium hydroxide. Scents and colors are added to make the soap more attractive to use.

MAKING A POWERED BOAT

You will need

✔ A large bowl of water
✔ A matchstick
✔ Detergent
✔ Scissors
✔ Foil

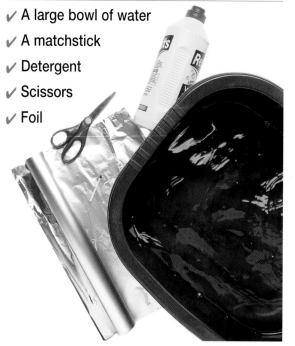

1 Flatten a piece of foil about 2 in (5 cm) square. Squeeze the foil between two books to make sure it is quite flat.

2 Cut a boatlike shape from the foil, with a small notch in the middle of the "stern." Smooth out the boat again.

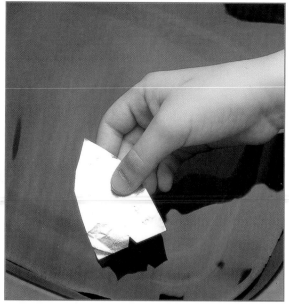

3 Fill the bowl with water, and lower the boat gently onto the surface. Surface tension will keep your foil boat floating.

What is happening?

When detergent is added to water, it breaks the surface tension and spreads quickly out across the surface of the water. When you place the detergent in the notch of your boat, the notch stops the detergent from spreading out. So the detergent thrusts the boat along instead.

Using a matchstick, gently drop a small drop of detergent into the notch. Your boat should shoot away rapidly over the surface.

Experiments in Science

Science is about knowledge: it is concerned with knowing and trying to understand the world around us. The word comes from the Latin word, *scire*, to know.

In the early 17th century, the great English thinker Francis Bacon suggested that the best way to learn about the world was not simply to think about it, but to go out and look for yourself—to make observations and try things out. Ever since then, scientists have tried to approach their work with a mixture of observation and experiment. Scientists insist that an idea or theory must be tested by observation and experiment before it is widely accepted.

All the experiments in this book have been tried before, and the theories behind them are widely accepted. But that it is no reason why you should accept them. Once you have done all the experiments in this book, you will know the ideas are true not because we have told you so, but because you have seen for yourself.

All too often in science there is an external factor interfering with the result which the scientist just has not thought of. Sometimes this can make the experiment seem to work when it has not, as well as making it fail. One scientist conducted lots of demonstrations to show that a clever horse called Hans could count things and tap out the answer with his hoof. The horse was indeed clever, but later it was found that rather than counting, he was getting clues from tiny unconscious movements of the scientist's eyebrows.

This is why it is very important when conducting experiments to be as rigorous as you possibly can. The more casual you are, the more "eyebrow factors" you will let in. There will always be some things that you can not control. But the more precise you are, the less these are likely to affect the outcome.

What went wrong?

However careful you are, your experiments may not work. If so, you should try to find out where you went wrong. Then repeat the experiment until you are absolutely sure you are doing everything right. Scientists learn as much, if not more, from experiments that go wrong as those that succeed. In 1929, Alexander Fleming discovered the first antibiotic drug, penicillin, when he noticed that a bacteria culture he was growing for an experiment had gone moldy—and that the mold seemed to kill the bacteria. A poor scientist would probably have thrown the moldy culture away. A good scientist is one who looks for alternative explanations for unexpected results.

Glossary

Atoms: Every substance is made of invisibly tiny atoms, which are the smallest particle of any chemical element. Each atom has a nucleus, around which minute electrons whirl.

Boiling point: Temperature at which a liquid turns into a gas. At normal atmospheric pressure pure water boils at 212°F (100°C).

Buoyancy: The ability of an object to float.

Condensation: The process by which water vapor turns into liquid water.

Density: The amount of a substance (mass) in a certain volume; a measure of how tightly packed the material is.

Electron: A tiny particle that whizzes around the nucleus of an atom. It has a negative electrical charge.

Evaporation: The process by which liquid water turns into water vapor.

Freezing point: Temperature at which a liquid turns into a solid. Pure water freezes at 32°F (0°C) at normal atmospheric pressure.

Hydroelectric power: Electricity that is made by the force of water power.

Hydrogen bond: Special bonds that hold water molecules together. They are caused by an attraction between the oxygen ions in one water molecule and the hydrogen ions in another water molecule.

Ion: An atom or molecule that has lost or gained an electron. An ion has a positive or a negative electrical charge, while an atom is neutral.

Irrigation: To supply cropland with extra water; it is mainly used in hot, dry countries.

Plimsoll line: Marks on the side of a ship that show the safe level to which the ship can be loaded.

Polar molecules: Molecules with slightly negative parts and slightly positive parts. Water is an example of a polar molecule.

Relative density: The density of a substance in relation to the density of pure water.

Salinity: A measure of how much salt is dissolved in a volume of water.

Surface tension: The force that forms across the surface of a body of water because of the attractions between water molecules.

Swimbladder: An air-filled sac inside the body of many types of fish. By filling the sac with air, or by squeezing air out of it, fish can control their buoyancy.

Upthrust: The force that pushes up against an object when the object is placed in a fluid such as water. An object floats if its weight is the same as the upthrust. It sinks if the upthrust cannot support its weight.

Index

A, B

Archimedes 19
Archimedes' Principle 19
boiling point 7, 31
buoyancy 18, 19, 31

C, D

Cavendish, Henry 5
clouds 11
convection currents 22, 23
Dead Sea 20
drought 11

E, F

evaporation 11, 31
freshwater 10, 11

G, H

glacier 10
heavy water 22
human need for water 4, 11
hydroelectric power 14, 15
hydrogen 5, 8
hydrogen bond 7, 8, 31
hydrological cycle 11
hydrology 11
hydrometer 24, 25

I, J, K, L

ice 7, 8, 9, 23
iceberg 7
iron 7
irrigation 12, 31
lakes 4, 10

M

melting point (of ice) 7

N, O

nuclear power 22
oceans 4, 10, 11, 23
  currents 23
oxygen 5, 8

P, Q

Plimsoll lines 24
polar molecule 8, 31
pump 13

R

rain 10, 11
rivers 4, 10

S

siphon 12
ships 19, 25
snow 10, 11
soap and detergent 27, 28, 29
steam 6
surface tension 26, 27, 29, 31
swimbladder 19, 31

U

upthrust 19, 21, 31

W

water, chemical formula 5
watermill 15
water molecule 5, 7, 8, 26, 27
water pressure 13, 14, 15, 16, 17
water vapor 6, 7, 10, 11